THE
MULCH
PILE
AND OTHER POEMS

THE
MULCH
PILE
AND OTHER POEMS

ROBERT W.
NERO

Illustrations by James A. Carson

NATURAL HERITAGE / NATURAL HISTORY INC.

Published by Natural Heritage/Natural History Inc.
P.O. Box 95, Station O, Toronto, Ontario M4A 2M8

Canadian Cataloguing in Publication Data

Nero, Robert W., 1922-
The mulch pile and other poems

ISBN 0-920474-83-7

I. Title

PS8577.E58M8 1993 C811'.54 C93-095284-7
PR9199.3.N47M8 1993

Design by Norton Hamil Design
Illustrations by James A. Carson

Natural Heritage/Natural History Inc. gratefully acknowledges the financial
assistance of the Ontario Arts Council. The support of the Government of
Ontario through the Ministry of Culture, Tourism and Recreation, and the assis-
tance of The Canada Council are also acknowledged.

INTRODUCTION

Few would notice a moth clinging to the pavement of an early
morning parking lot. Fewer still would pause, stoop delighted to
examine it and then carefully carry it to safety among the nearby
foliage. Robert Nero, having marvelled at the delicate creature
and guarded it to share with a friend, vividly describes the event in
a brief poem, *Night's Debris*.

Who would notice an eight-foot long single strand spider's web
catching the clustered flakes of a late April snowfall, laughing with
delight when new flakes set the silken strand aswinging? Nero's
poem, *April Miracle* so successfully captures the event that one wishes
to have been there to share in the wonder of it.

The *Mulch Pile* brings together a collection of poetry from the
pen of prairie writer/naturalist Robert Nero. Like his earlier book,
Woman By the Shore, it is rather like an album of snapshots to leaf
through...here is Bob walking the dog; here in the garden with
Ruth; here pensively watching from his window. Each poem is
carefully crafted to reveal the essence of one event and his appre-
ciation of it.

There is no sweeping grandeur here; these are personal vignettes.
Each poem captures a poet's impressions with startling clarity.
Each thoughtfully chosen word contributes to a quiet eloquence
which pervades the entire volume. Oaks do indeed bear "green
lacquered leaves", though one may never have seen them that way
without Nero's help. Each poem is itself "a momentary gem" in a
mulch pile of tiny treasures.

It is a great pleasure to welcome this second book of poetry by
Robert Nero. Readers of *The Mulch Pile* will appreciate the subjects
of these collected poems as well as the artistry of their presentation.

Ardythe McMaster

CONTENTS

City Streets

Country Views

THE
MULCH
PILE
AND OTHER POEMS

FOREWORD

"Compost heap" is probably a more accurate term than "mulch pile", but long before composting was fashionable we called our backyard pile of leaves the leaf pile and, then, after we began digging out the old decomposed material, we called it the mulch pile. We now harvest mulch annually. The leaves grow and fall, are gathered and placed in the mulch pile and from there enrich our garden. Thus is life renewed.

Like the mulch pile, the human mind collects a lot of miscellaneous items. Given time, a settling takes place, a kind of natural regeneration. New thoughts are born, perhaps even a poem. Sometimes a felicitous line will emerge as surprisingly as a lost plastic toy in our mulch pile.

Our city lot measure 23 by 81 metres. It's a fairly well-treed lot in a rustic part of Winnipeg. A small piece at the back with a few aspen and oak trees remains in an almost natural state. In miniature, it constitutes a complex community of living things that one will never get to know completely.

Coming home from some errand or outing is like coming into a small park. Although we live close to a busy thoroughfare, our yard is a haven. Oh, occasionally we get tired of yardwork; every year the trees and shrubs require more attention, and my wife sometimes gets tired of raking up leaves.

Publication in May 1990 of a book of poems: *Woman By The Shore*, gave me immense satisfaction and motivated me to keep writing. That book was published as a tribute to Louise de Kiriline Lawrence. Louise died April 27, 1992 at age 98. I'm pleased to dedicate this collection to her memory. The last piece of writing by Louise appeared in the March 1985 Audubon magazine: *A Springtime Affair* is not only a delightful exposition of the nature of the ruffed grouse, it also has a poetical expressiveness. That was the special talent of Louise Lawrence.

I am indebted to Elizabeth Morton for critically reviewing several poems and to Betty Struthers for providing typing skills along with more than one cup of tea. Thanks are also due Margaret Belcher for editorial assistance, and Ardythe McMaster for the gracious introduction. I am enormously grateful to Jim Carson for his sketches, some of which are poems in themselves.

As with *Woman By The Shore*, *The Mulch Pile* owes much to publisher Barry Penhale, his wife Jane, and daughter Nancy, for their encouragement and support.

Without the constant care of our home and yard by my wife, Ruth F. Nero, whose steadfast loyalty and love have enriched my life, it is unlikely that these poems would have happened.

Robert W. Nero

ONE MAN'S LOT

THE MULCH PILE

More goes into our mulch pile
than leaves
we've discovered
so we sift the old stuff
through a screen
picking out sticks and stones
and assorted artifacts
a pleasant autumn chore
archaeology of a kind.

There's an astonishing variety
of plastic scraps
shreds of containers, thin, thick
black, green and clear
from where does it come?
of course it never goes
blown on the wind
lost in the night.

A scary piece of sharp glass
seems more friendly
though not for my wife's garden;
a shiny blue glass marble
brings a smile to us both
and whose treasure was this
tiny red plastic bird?

The sifted mulch falls gently
in the wheelbarrow
rich and dark it makes a
growing heap beside the garden
a mountain where centipedes and
sowbugs scramble for a foothold
slithering, falling
digging in out of the light.

While I worked
my sore back aching
six robins gathered
stood about silently, watching
then flew down to rummage
on the soft humus hill
starting small landslides
each time they pounced on prey
all of us feeling fall.

SEASON'S END

Troops of quiet grackles
so black on a cloudy morning
move across our lawn
in search of sustenance
prying open curled oak leaves
balancing acorns in open bills
the short tails of some
a sign of change as
families and individuals merge
in compact flocks
social gatherings that
surprise and delight us
spelling an end to summer...
they drift along with
the same magic as the golden
leaves falling from our birch.

SEPTEMBER MONARCH

This butterfly that silently
floats by us can see and
steer and sail all the way
to Mexico, those parchment wings
carrying it
across highways, rivers
mountains, deserts...
for now it's content to
drink from our fall flowers
approaching with an elegant
dainty attitude that belies
its power...it glides past us
on set wings, wafting, its
monarchial colours well suited
to this hot, humid Labour Day.
It drifts through our yard
with majestic spirit
a touch of hope for summer
between the trees, in and
out of the carport
its solemn mien
gracing this place.
How lucky we are, I think
to have such a bright creature
to show us the way.
I wish it well, thinking
uncomfortably of those
torrential highways
steamy parking lots
all the ways a butterfly
can meet an unseemly end—
with any luck we'll see you
in spring, or one of your kind.

AUTUMN SOUNDS

Standing beside my car
in early morning
listening to robins
singing soft songs
wheedling whispers
muted calls that suit
the autumn mood...
suddenly I realized that
their voices masked the
noise of nearby traffic
and I was glad for
wild birds.

THE COLOUR OF OAKS

I didn't know
that oaks were ever pink
until one cold November day
I saw their uppermost limbs
aloft against a
pale lavender sky
still as silence
lit by rosy dawn.

FLICKER'S FEATHER

I have a fondness for flickers
the way they come down from trees
to crouch and stab the lawn
gravely poking holes in the sod
probing the earth for ants.

They look so vulnerable there
in their serious searching
black bib lowered to ground
deepening their shadowed front
blazing head lifting to scan.

Rump feathers shining white
wings trembling with excitement
face down, pausing, drawing up
reluctant frenzied ants on tongue
our flicker hurriedly feasts.

Sometimes they sprawl in the sun
head tilted back to face the sky
bill open to receive the heat
resting upon spread wings
a temporary lull in a busy life.

When I find a golden shaft
atilt on the green grass
shed in summer's passing
I take it as a gift to cherish
a flicker's toll fully paid.

SATURDAY MORNING

Sliding on the wet lawn
in my old moosehide moccasins,
red bathrobe flapping,
like some kid on a rink
while my wife watches warily
from her window seat
on this cloudy October morning
my breath visible
but the cold wind down and
a gentle calm prevailing.

I'd go barefoot to feel fall
between my toes and shiver a bit
but for her pleas to ease
my arthritic joints and
avoid our neighbors' eyes;
as it is, feel a lump of clay
impressed upon one sole
which no amount of sliding
can dislodge so, chastened,
stop and scrape away some
garden soil lost among the leaves.

After breakfast in bed (her treat)
we jostle in the kitchen and hug
recalling last week's unseemly
anger (all mine, for no good reason)—
I list my frets, stumble
over words and emotions, settle
on minor chores, use the phone
look up to see her bending beside me
gathering thin leaves off the rug...
she holds them out for my inspection
then teasingly asks: "Souvenirs?"

RAINY NOVEMBER DAY

This may be my last walk
on grass this year
so I tread lovingly
feeling a softness underfoot
a resiliency of merit
something to remember
through the long winter
coming tonight.

These damp leaves blown
across our clean lawn
were torn off the willows
by the wind that
brought rain and
now is pulling in snow.

Mark my steps well
these faded lawn colours
pale umber, thin yellow
almost green suddenly seem
precious compared to snow
our grass waiting for cover
to keep the cold aloft
until awakening spring.

So I walk with care
stepping over tree roots
left spread like fingers
this dry fall's legacy
a pattern of drought
hardly relieved by one
November rain I forgot
to walk in, another regret.

MORNING RUN

Our winter-loving dog
enjoys his brief outing
dashing around the yard
with pure delight
he leaps, turns to sniff,
runs, thrusts himself
between trees and under shrubs
plunges into a snowdrift
bounds out with a great leap
then nimbly skips around
an icy patch on the trail.

His energetic quick-footedness
reminds me of youthful days
when I too exuberantly cavorted
celebrating spring by
running down hills with abandon
jumping over rocks and gullies
confidently trusting to gravity
and agile feet to see me
safely home...
now I only smile and
watch the dog run.

WEATHER BREAK

Shoveling fresh snow on a
late December morning
I stopped for an unexpected
bird sound, a slurred trill...
only chirping house sparrows
a "cluck" from our lone grackle
so what had I heard?
back to shoveling, then again
a squeaky, hesitant trill
our grackle with spread tail
essaying song!
having survived several chill
nights at forty below
he's feeling good for much
the same reason as me
this mild morning and blue sky
lifting our spirits.

SAMARAS

The winged fruits of
our Manitoba maple
still hang suspended
this bright February day
multiple clusters glittering
straw-gold against
a pale blue sky
shivering in the breeze
a decorative touch that
softens crooked black branches.
I'd want no better view
from my bed were I dying
than these faded unfallen fruits
that catch thin fire
from sunlight.

SPARROWS CHIRPED AT AUSCHWITZ

Despite the cries of shame and despair
the sun rose at dawn
a shaft of light breaking through
morose clouds low in the sky
warming a gray rooftop where
sparrows hopped and chirped
their familiar pearly "sureep"
unannounced by loudspeaker's
raucous hoot, more compelling
to my ear than soundman knew...
I wept before our TV screen
knowing that sparrows
chirped at Auschwitz
just the same.

TASTE TEST

This morning I ate some snow
while walking in our grove of trees
feeling for the trail beneath new snow
came to the one spruce where you need
to stoop a little to get by
there stopped to admire snow on a bough
at face-level, soft masses, gently rounded
by sun, lovely, froth-like so
leaned to take a soft bite
a mouthful of cold dryness crystalline
melting against tongue and palate
a trace of water to swallow
and again, a deeper bite
as I've seen our dog do
the same studied savoring thinking
so that's what it's like
the dog and I sharing sensations
that every little kid already knows.

MARCH DANCE

Outside my window a chickadee
is seeking spiders
fluttering like a slow hummingbird
hovering beneath our thin-lipped
maple seeds clustered on the ends of twigs
moving from one frond to another
to find prey warmed by morning light
or what else moves spiders
to come out from winter lair
on a cold morning in spring?

Why this frantic searching when
the feeders are filled with seeds that
fed chickadees all winter, I wonder
or is there some goodness in spiders
some sweet taste that lingers
that makes a bird go searching
dancing in the air with sunlight
split through fast feathers
a splash of light, dangling an instant
faster than I can reach for pen...
a momentary gem.

VIEWPOINT

I didn't know
that when my wife
sat quietly knitting
she was seeing a small girl
in a blue sweater walking
into the future.

I didn't know
that she found relief
from cares and worries
in the steady slip of yarn
and flow of bright colour
through her hands.

So thoughtfully caring
were those women
who sat by fires in caves
crafting children's garments
from animal skins.

SPRING THAW WITH OWL

Any bird that measures the
fall of a drop of water
studiously peering down at
the soft plink in the snow
then briefly glancing up
as if daring me to criticize
merits a lot of respect.

WEST WINDOW

The evening sky rests
on a small meltwater pool
beneath our backyard trees
an artful reflection
I almost missed
lying in bed beneath depression.
Now the trees are blocking out the light
and the pool is soaking up the dark...
fast, fast night is over us
a heavy long silence except a
distant dog barking and our
spaniel at my feet
sighing in his sleep.

Now the pool is gone though
if I walked out there I bet
I'd see it still swinging by
I'd better hurry, it may be gone
by dawn.

OPPORTUNITY LOST

Just as the sun was setting
you said something about
catkins on the lawn..."I know,
I know" I exclaimed, "the aspen
catkins are all coming down."
Then I looked up to find low
sunlight illuminating catkins
lying on the lawn.
"I wonder what makes them
glow that bright" I asked
pondering that so much light
should shine from each, and
thought to run out quick
to crouch low to better see
what made them glow so...but
when next I looked up they were
gone, the light done, evening fast—
now the rain has pressed them flat
into the grass like bits of flannel,
another chance missed.

CONTRAST

I celebrate spring
gathering in the image of new
aspen catkins against a high blue sky
with scattered clouds sailing by,
standing still to hear a junco's trill
above the traffic's roar,
making note of the precise angle
at which a robin's head is tilted
to catch the morning sun;
Ruth celebrates the warm day
kneeling upright at her garden
upon the smooth dun lawn
counting green leaves unveiled
with rake and no-nonsense fingers,
planning flower beds and bees
to bring summer into being...
there is a happy humming in the air
her fresh smile and wind-tossed hair
vie with a flicker's familiar stance
as it stolidly punctures the lawn
to bring up wriggling ants...
in this moment we silently sing.

SUDDEN URGE

I thought I'd chosen winter
as my favorite time of year
feeling sad to see the snow go
dismayed by all the grass and birds
appearing overnight too soon
but then I stretched upon the lawn
eyes closed, sun warm on my face
let my shoulders back and felt
the ground pressing up to meet me
a restful embrace I'd forgotten;
so lovers yield to springtime
falling back upon the grass
lulled by earth's fervent turning.

THE OWL'S GIFT

In the dark rainy night
I consult with this oracle
reaching through soft feathers
to feel her warm throat
thinking as I do that
the fabric of her being
is mere thin skin stretched
over braced bones and flesh
a fragile assemblage
to so command our attention.
So then where's the spirit of
this comforting creature that
ceaselessly charms us all?
It must be in her mind
(do birds have minds?)
it's in her attitude, the way
she trusts and accepts us;
she comes from her owl-being
to meet us in her time
gravely allowing us a
glimpse of her world
a gift of tender tolerance
we do well to honour.

NEW ARRIVALS

The thrushes are back!
I exclaimed to you
holding out for inspection
a chalk-white casting such
as sprinkled the lawn
in numbers last April,
a puzzle to resolve until
I matched droppings with
faint fluted call...
crushed on my finger
a close look reveals
shiny fragments of insects
an incredible feat this
catching of beetles
so early in spring...
where do they find so many
creatures to gulp as treats
snow being only days behind?
In dark, leafy corners
they prowl quietly
tipping over damp debris
with nimble bills and
quick moist tongues...
a savory feast.

APRIL VISITOR

Our lame grackle survived
the dark numb nights
of January and February
watched the snow melt
enjoyed the freedom of
bare ground and dry lawn
met the first juncos—
then disappeared.

We wondered why sparrows
that used to crowd the feeder
cowered under shrubs
came warily to feed
then darted back in hiding,
even the blue jays seemed
strangely silent.

Early this cloudy morning
a gray shadow slipped silently
through branches of the oak
to boldly perch above the feeder,
upright, raptor eyes gleaming—
"Sharp-shin!" I called...
we watched this marauder
bobbing its fine head
as it searched for prey,
then it skimmed off
on quick wings.

We guessed the hawk had
been here before, the
grackle's thin flesh
food to speed those migrant wings
through urban lots to finer woods
where sharp-shins call,
leaving our sparrows wary still
that fierce image yet
a presence in our quiet yard.

FIRST FLOWERS

The crows are calling
out the aspen flowers
their silver bursts
cry spring
from every crooked twig
against the sky,
those buds that swelled
that split with down
one mild winter day
now tremble with new sap;
slow down, I think
remembering how easily
those furry catkins are
dashed to ground
their male seeds shed
upon the silent green
female flowers waiting
on nearby trees—
a pageant of sexuality
marking every spring.

APRIL PAGEANT

Suddenly I find
lush aspen catkins
like fingers of light
their massed hands
gathering sunlight to
brighten shadowed woods
a triumph of spring...
we should be dancing in
the streets to celebrate
this glorious awakening
of our native trees
with flowers that delight
for a few days
astonishingly fragile clusters
of blossoms gone wild
with fresh sap rising
to the sun's urge...
they are so soon gone
dashed down by wind
and rain or late snow.

APRIL MIRACLE

In a mid-April fall of snow
we watched the lawn whitening
beneath a dark sullen sky
a constant falling of flakes
that drew our eyes down,
a quiet fall that stilled birds,
and then you saw a spider's web
a single strand reaching eight feet
from eave to tree suspended—
it caught your eye because
it was catching snow, huge
clustered flakes that weighed
the line down until it bowed
and there at midline flakes
met and melted, congealed
silvered pearl that brought
the silk strand lower still.
We laughed together to see
some flakes strike the line in
passing, set it swinging, and
then some adhered and slid downhill,
from right and left clustered
flakes rode the line in steep descent
a thrilling passage of unforeseen
wonder to keep us watching
until with too much weight
the line broke, a web lost...
a gift to see us through an
April snowfall.

FINALLY IT'S SPRING

I'm outside, bareheaded
thin snow blankets
vibrating in the warm sun
retreating, making pools
where images of trees
give surprising depth
to our yard, patterns
keener than I'd remembered
a natural joy, providing
the water stays on the lawn
and not in the basement.
Our small rock pile reappears
reminding me that at least
one smooth chipmunk lies
beneath, nose to tail
curled up in its den
or slowly blinking?
feeling the warmth perhaps
a faint stirring, awakening
to spring's caress.
A faint humming in my ears
loud against the pure hush
of this calm poised day
a quality of light, a clarity
I'd forgotten.
Our garden emerging
the melting snow crystal lace
driven by sun's high rays
fragile surface gleaming
intact until touched
the beauty of decaying snow
the black soil velvet-smooth.

LATE SNOW

It's enough to break my wife's heart
to see the lawn all white with snow
her garden stakes in rows
where lettuce seeds huddle below,
but I find solace in winter in spring
discover grey aspen catkins draped
on twigs like wet fox furs,
stand silent in the hush of
falling snow and hear a dove's
soft call who knows it's spring
despite the cold, and gulls cry
overhead appear on silent wings
sweet apparitions, artful things,
it's winter all over again
except for all these tender leaves sprung from
furious buds—
hold fast, I think, all leaves
and flowers, please stay still
this won't last, though the soft
swelled green lilac bursts
seem numb with surprise,
so many silent leaves I'd not
seen growing now glow green
against pure white—
even the lawn delights:
all those new upright blades
above the snow making a landscape
of miniature trees in which a
silent robin slowly hops,
and mark a warbler's wet wings
as it flutters up beneath a low bough
solemnly prowling at my feet who
usually search at loftier heights,
my wife watches from the window
as the dog and I weave trails—

ah, love, your sunny disposition
will see you through, your flowers
yet will bloom, the juncos, siskins
all these new summer birds
wait with you for sunny bliss.

MAY LAMENT

One can't afford to miss
a day of spring,
I thought, suddenly aware
that the oak flowers
were done, flowers
that held my eye for days
as they descended from
bare hard twigs
pendant small sprays
palest green tendrils
expressed from corky twigs
before a sign of a leaf—
flowers that after sunset
crowned our oaks with
a curious light, a hint
of palest salmon against
the darkening sky
some resonance of fallen sun
or quarter-moon's glow
enough to make me bring
my wife running to see
how oaks hold song—
suddenly they're done
dry, shriveled, no longer limp
but bent, breaking off
a sad going, brushed

from tops of cars
swept along curbs...
who cares for May flowers
dares not sleep.

MAY LAMENT - SEQUEL

Those delicate oak flowers
that dried and shriveled
to wiry beards all seemed
doomed to fall, but now
in June I find some
still on their twigs
hidden beneath green
lacquered oak leaves
grown overnight it seems...
not lost at all
having caught the spirit
they're just humming away in
expectation of autumn surprise
nurturing oak seeds,
those remarkable growths,
capped numb fruits
burnished acorns that
fall on our roof like stones
that feed our many squirrels
that sprout all over our yard...
I'm amazed, having lived
with oaks for years
I thought I knew how
acorns grew—
another lesson learned.

WHOOPS!

I watched a bumblebee
foraging on your first flowers,
it clambered up the underside
and over the top of an orange poppy
determinedly thrust its head
through golden pollen to
claim the sweet bounty,
flew directly into another
lacking such goodness
judging by its hasty exit
then, best of all, it
dipped down toward a yellow
fallen poppy petal
before it realized its mistake
and went whizzing off to the lilacs.

NEW TENANT

No robins used the platform
we'd installed under the eave
remembering how the squirrels
stole their eggs last year
but now I see a spider's
taken over with drafting
precise as stars, spun out
a web against the sun
a silken sail fitted between
robin's ledge and eave
one night's work to
catch a fly
no birdsong now, but
an orb-weaver's craft
silently shimmering
a dawnsong.

SLEIGHT OF HAND

Summer came out of spring
almost overnight it seemed
fully sprung from
hesitant beginnings
a time-warp burst of opulence
to frustrate those of us
who like to count the steps
from one season to another.

I meant to measure the
growth of oak flowers
but they've already burst forth
frothy jade-green hangings
covering bare hard twigs
with oriental finery.
We watched the swelling buds
saw catkins uncoil and hang
from aspen, birch and alder
enjoyed the immodest pink outcry
of flowering crab trees
saw warblers duck through
massed white apple blossoms
startling mating mourning doves
that we had watched walking slowly
atop May's last snow.

Now suddenly there are leaves
on every tree I see
leaves atop the oak flowers
young aspen leaves fluttering
moving boughs aslant the wind,
our wild plum's ecstatic flowers
have shrunk back for leaves
and robins stand on lush lawns.
Birds subdued by heady warmth
and all this sudden growth
slip silently through shrubs
imbued with greenery where
only days before red stems gleamed,
now the brightest birds
can hide amidst leafy green and gold
absorbed by summer's drapery.

The world is turning green at last
from plush shorn lawns gleaming
against the toll of lawn machines
to trees grown great against
the sky where martins dip and glean.

There is a scent of foliage
a husky essence upon the air
dripping from leaves gone mad
astonishing splendor that
turns pale sunlight green,
even the shadows are green.

WILD ROSE

Incredible that
this black earth
should produce
such scented pink.

OWL BATHING

She dips her head
and drinks
drinks again
peers over one shoulder
abruptly hops in
studies her reflection
looks around casually
lurches forward
onto her breast
with an embarrassed look
then, with a sigh, commits:
thrusts out her broad wings
thrashes violently—
for that moment she's
an ordinary bird
a robin, a sparrow...
in such quick immersion
they hold their fears
and bathe.

SUMMER EVENING

Morning-glory flowers
furled against August heat
at evening fall limply
as quietly as soft kisses
a gentle relinquishment
of their day of splendor.

AUGUST BOON

Bits of tan and rose fluff
like colorful pills pulled
off a wool sweater
appear unexpectedly
beneath the oak trees,
littering lawn-chairs,
sprinkled on the grass
wherever there are oaks,
furry blooms bursting forth
from whitened oak leaves
inspired by dancing gall-flies
whose silent larvae turning
within exotic galls
in an underleaf world
send down this gay confetti—
a celebration of summer.

BOTANY LESSON

I hadn't realized
what artful arrangement
of floral parts
our wild iris bore
until I watched a bee
burrowing down inside the length
of blue recurved petals.

HASTY REACTION

Cleaning an outside window
high on a stepladder
you discovered wasps
driving you down to protect
their impeccable nest
tucked under the eave...
odd we hadn't noticed it.

I happily sprayed the nest
in an unfriendly way
then scraped it down,
thin grey paper layers
waxen cells with blind
pupae flexing their torsos;
so much care and effort,
puzzled wasps returning
all evening—I suppose
we could have left it.

THE ACORN MINE

Now in January's true cold
my walk in our little woods
on a path hard as stone
is more hurried than usual
glasses frosted over
rims stinging my cheeks
as I peer over the top but look what I find:
a medley of tracks in the snow
where there's been a diligent
tunneling down to last fall's
harvest of unwanted acorns
raked from our lawn repeatedly
hauled to rest in a great heap
a bounty too solid to mulch
left for squirrels to pillage
red squirrels mining fruit
to brighten their coats
burrowing down through snow
from three directions
bringing up ore all winter long
shaft openings littered
with scattered tailings
acorn caps and husks strewn
for rabbits to munch
the brown burnished hulls
and bits of grass reminding me
on the instant of those pleasant
days when acorns fell like stones
rattling on the roof and
roughening our lawn in fall ...
the grass soft and smooth.

FIRST FALL WARBLER

A thump against the window
something fluttering amongst
my wife's cosmos below...
carefully parting the flowers
I find a stunned small warbler
palest green, mouth open
bright eyes quivering and
a heart beating too fast
a fragile form to hold,
all its history in my hand
whatever days it knew in
humid bog and family ties
brought to this moment...
thinking it's too early
for fall migrants, then,
glancing at my wristwatch
realized it was already August
a late date for birds who
appear even in July to
announce a summer waning...
when the warbler thrust against
my fingers I held it up
to freedom, watched it slipping
through spruce boughs
a slight thing, a Tennessee
back in its world.

PARTNERS

My old dog silently
watches me eating cookies
upright posture, ears alert
warm brown eyes steady
on my face...
behaviour formed ages ago
by lean hunting dogs waiting
beside fires for a piece of
the hard-earned kill.

FIRST ICE

Watching a blue jay
fly to the bird bath
for a drink...
as it landed
it slipped on the new ice
wings out for balance
it stopped in surprise
puzzledly tapped the ice
then turned to fly
again losing its balance
as its feet slid back—
a lesson learned
this cold October morning.

NO WREN THIS YEAR

Stand still to listen
in the wet grass and shadows
of early morning calm
missing our wren's fervent song
that filled our yard and
drew shy mates in every year;
there's the nuthatch calling,
a blue jay's shrill cry, and
the oriole's double flute-note
but, oh, I miss the wren ...
he seemed a permanent fixture
as dependable as the wild rose
now crowning wren's thickets;
the traffic noise seems louder
in the absence of wren song
and the empty wren houses gloom.

CITY STREETS

ADVENT

A few yellow leaves
swirling on the pavement
downed by August heat
enough to evoke
a feeling of fall.

ANNOUNCEMENT

Suddenly it begins!
a firestorm of yellow
that lifts me up—
across the green banks
of young aspen trees
overnight appears
the golden glow that
heralds autumn—
true, this dry season
plays a part in
the turning, but
now's the time
when green goes out
and our aspens shout
gold across woods
along streams, in groves
in clumps and single trees
but, oh, this massed effect:
aspen woods shining forth
a crowd of upright flags
suspended in a calm
bright sea of new colour.

WARM NOVEMBER MORNING

Though hunched over my desk
in my mind
I am walking in this morning's fog
stepping softly amongst damp leaves
delighting in a sense of spring
in a late November "warm air mass"
there is this dark silence
hushed traffic sliding by
I'd run out if I could
to find a damp hawk moodily staring
at its toes
catch some pearly light I'd never
seen before in fogged windows
listen to the tinkle of ice
on the river beyond the shore
smile at people by the bus stop
peering at their watches...
the grass will have to remember for me,
since I have work to do,
how dew gathered last
before surrendering to cold.

SEASONAL ITEM

When I see fall muskrats
flattened on the street
I know it's not long
before the first snow.

A burnished brown and grey
a softness, shape and size that
makes them easy to spot
even when ground flat.

We rarely see them running
they must trot along at night
forced to move by low water
or too many of their kind.

Not so much carcasses as furs
their remains recall marsh scenes
river edges, giving the city
a welcome touch of wildness.

BRISK WINTER WALK

Each walk I take leads to new surprises
even when I walk the same trail,
in the woods find junk heaps softened
by last night's bountiful snow
trash turned into appealing abstract art
stop to admire again the multiple
star-bursts of dill grown wild
nibbling on a few dry seeds
to taste their sweet tartness
like any wild creature seeking comfort,
wondering if deer whose prints I follow
ever stop to sample more than twigs,
heads turned to listen, rolling
new flavors on their tongues,
are they listening now, I wonder?
as I desperately blow my cold nose
carefully pocketing sodden tissue
for not even in the snow will I
allow myself the ease of thoughtless
scatter, having made my own rules
long ago, and forced them on our kids
who fondly recall the scoldings
falling on young ears like thunder
dad gone all furious over that word
so new then, littering, he said;
on the return trip feel tightening thighs
and labored breath, my dog moving faster
heading home than I desire
so loose the leash and watch him trot off
hind quarters moving on a separate line
like some automobile needing alignment,
lights in windows gleaming
this pre-Christmas evening...

are there people watching this 68-year
old man walking his 8-year old dog?
and wave friendly greetings to drivers
who slow to pass man and dog now on
the run, a burst of speed (though short)
to thrill tired lungs and legs, but still
gather in the sight of three starlings
planing through trees to land
like urchins in a row, wings tucked in
against the cold, quiet as puffs of smoke
eyes pivoting I suppose, then off they go again;
the shoveled driveways, multiple parked cars
or often empty yards express a festive
burst of activity, visiting
building new relationships
a bringing together of friends, family,
even foes, to still the night
to bind delight into holidays
another year's chance to set things right.

IN BETWEEN TIME

Winter is so brown until it's white
a sad sight
leafless trees with bare branches
upright arms against the sky
a time of withering
brown leaves rattling
across the brown grass;
now colour comes from
kids' clothes, toques
jackets bright as rain
scarves, boots...
even lipstick sings
a praise to colour.

WINTER SURPRISE

Driving by evening woods
I discovered a ballet
with near trees
swinging rhythmically
past distant trees,
an astonishing feat,
varying their pace as
I slowed down or
sped past—
and all for free I
thought, pleased to tell
tree shapes against a
twilight sky:
oaks a little bristly
with fine twigs
aspens crooked candelabra
spruce momentous dark
ash trees reaching high
all turning on some
remote axis
a dance to delight
tired eyes.

DECEMBER MORN

There is a grace
achieved through attitude
a warm glow across the mind
that brings light to
night's dark despair,
I have it now
so rise with dawn
to walk the dog.
In this new mood
enjoy the blush of
rounded flanks of aspen trunks
wrapped with sun
note bunched fruits of
ornamental crabs clinging
to crooked branches
a feast for birds to come
stop enthralled when a hairy
woodpecker drums, that quick
beat measuring its gaiety.
My dog pulls and I resist,
needing a longer look at
furred goldenrod seedheads
not yet in the sun
and even find pleasure in the
warm colour of old rusted buckets
items I'd otherwise scorn.
A full stop to ponder clustered
rose hips, fine lights ignited
on their shiny red coats,
brown hazel leaves margined
with frost, suspended in silence
vole holes punched through snow
pointy two-toed prints of deer
a squirrel's fine chatter.

I draw from these to
quicken my step, shoulders back
looking up and around –
alive at last.

TREES OF WINTER

The trees of winter
stand forth against the
evening sky
leafless boughs arranged in ways
I've never seen till now
shameless naked limbs
entwined: oaks, elms, ash
all reaching for the sky
fine lines etched in black
on twilight's lavender fall
intricate patterns I've seen before
but now I see them better
they ring new bells
delight my eyes—
the evening draws down fast
these December days
a limpid darkening sky of
opalescent washed folds
with charcoal streaks to close
I'm left with delicate traceries of
frost-white boughs under
street lamps' glow
and sombre spruce beyond
a solemn note to spy...

the trees hold dominion
over earth and sky, and I...
I travel on.

FEBRUARY SURPRISE

One glimpse of cattails
in a city ditch
is all it takes to
lift my spirits high,
those upright stalks
against the snow provide
a pageant of grace:
lean lines as brown
as toast, a cinnamon feast
for tired eyes
bladed leaves and spears
held high against
all winter's fury,
more compelling than
a traffic light that
moves me away, but
one more glance
to stake a claim
to uncut cattails
in an urban drain.

WALKING ON THE OUTSIDE

Today the dog and I,
lured out by mild weather,
walked two miles from home
(well, the dog went farther);
I went along for exercise
(trying to shake a foul mood)
suffering the dog's pull on the leash
halting when he sniffed, no, snuffled
at other dogs' dribbles beside the road;
we must have looked a proper pair
walking and trotting in tandem.
When we reached the woods
I slipped the dog's leash
to send him running off
in pursuit of exciting scents
while I marched down the path
coat open and hands bare
more quick-footed than usual.
I was hurrying home
almost out of the woods before
I realized my sorry state:
undiscerning, noting nothing
emotionally blind—
a futile walk in terms of feeling
coming back with less than burs
walking only on the outside.

MARCH THAW

Hold off, spring!
ease off this March warmth
I've not yet enjoyed winter enough
all those unfinished chores
and your puddles don't suit
our banks of clean white snow
still holding down the yard
against the grit of spring.
Oh, I'll admit some pleasure
in seeing lawns exposed where
sun lifted snow to sky
leaving grass shimmering
in afternoon light
like some fine fur,
even the dry street feels firm
beneath our wheels and
my open window belies my
wish for winter; I've half a mind
to drive north and hide again
beneath cruel cold and harsh wind;
I'm not yet ready for blackbirds.

INSIGHT

On a city street
a harried grackle
striving to attain
its destiny
urgently pursues
some prey item...
I drive past
on another journey.

MEMORY TRICK

For the friendly ear
the emphatic chirping of
a cock house sparrow
is easily heard above the
sound of city traffic;
compelled by familiarity
I stop and listen
my mind turning around
back more than fifty springs...
the same pleasant calls
beside a chicken coop
my Daisy BB-gun against
my cheek a strong connection
with wild birds...a seeming
contradiction
only a few birds lost.

DIVERSION

In the midst of a skirmish
between two chipping sparrows
the aggressor takes time off
to pursue a tempting moth.

HEMILYTRA

This strange feather
in a morning rain-pool
on the street
below the falcon nest
caught my eye—
lame back and all
I bent to pluck,
hesitated, not a feather?
but feather-like, a leaf?
unlike any leaf I've known
so stroked it dry
held it up to sun and stared
then smiled, this thin
leathery, leaf-like
feathery form familiar
a fragment detached
from its owner
a water-bug's fore-wing
its delicate, curved beauty
now easily perceived.
This falling through air
inspires wondrous shapes
an element of falcon's flight
found in feather and leaf
and insect wing.

NIGHT'S DEBRIS

This curious small object
in the parking lot—
an isosceles triangle in
white and cinnamon brown—
drew my attention,
a medallion? a lost badge?

With fuzzy morning eyes
I bent down closer and
found it alive! a moth!
its splendor breathtaking,
with cryptic pattern like a
computer-drawn wolf's face.

A fragile moth with
white sails folded
was clinging tightly to
the gritty pavement
its arrow shape pointing
into the morning wind.

I guarded the treasure
until you arrived,
your delight my reward,
feeling like an accomplice
as we carefully carried it
away to leafy shelter.

SENTINEL

Sturdy white cross
brooding by itself
alone in a snow-covered field
no tree, no shrub
not even weeds for company
only a wire fence
to keep out foxes
or the plow.

A poor grave that lacks a tree
I thought, wondering who
cultivated so close
and why...
though someone painted
the cross and
built the fence.

Perhaps the man's grave
who broke this land
a lifetime spent
knocking down trees
grubbing out stumps
making room for crops
and children...
surrounded by the open
space he craved.

THE CHASE

With true hunter's grace
a shrike atop a roadside willow
leaves with a flourish, darts
away along the snow-filled ditch
hovers over a weedy patch
then sails back to the same perch.
Seconds later a small dark object
comes out from the weeds
skitters across the fresh snow
a frightened mouse, I think
but no, some unknown thing like a
curled-up caterpillar
upright, blown by the wind
aerodynamically stable, rolling
down the road past the shrike...
will it strike, we wonder
but it simply watches silently
its eye more discerning than ours.
Curious by now, I jump out
to retrieve it, run down the
slippery road trying to block it
with one foot without stepping on it...
a strange chase—finally catch up
with it and pounce, then laugh
holding this tuft of brown fur
attached to thin dry skin
a bit of meadow mouse still
running with the wind
remnant of shrike's bounty...
of such fine parts am I now
enriching my life.

LUNCH BREAK

Wandering off the road on foot
away from the car and the CBC Radio
on a bright afternoon thinking:
this snowy field is all mine
for the walking in
I'll step wherever I please
plowing quietly through two
feet of powdery soft snow,
my wandering trail leaning a
little left to where a deer
crossed after last night's
fresh snow, a clean slate...
no hesitation in its trail
such being more sure of
their direction or need;
in this refreshed mood
slowing and puffing
stopped to enjoy crisp shadows
from every visible stalk and blade
chewing an apple while
adding up mouse tracks, holes
an abundance of sign where
owls hunt watching, listening—
this meadow so white and clean
where I could rest forever forlorn
beneath its taut surface
if I had the choice, a dream—
here hares on padded feet have stepped
boisterously, see where
one reached upwards to nip
a frozen twig, its great prints
softly spoken—

then, with childish elation,
carefully placed my apple core
at a vole's rounded doorway
noting urine stains and
small greenish droppings
where vole stopped and sniffed
the cold air before dawn
its thin whiskers twitching...
will it be surprised to find
and test my frozen apple core
I wondered, a tasty treat?
so stooped to study how clover
seeds cling to stem
suspended high above mice who
wait for deeper snow to reach;
on turning back I'm surprised
by my blue shadow's length
the time passing fast,
then leave, stepping new tracks
my brief sojourn expressed at last.

TREASURE HUNT

Up to my knees in clean snow
in a northern bog
carefully pawing open the
overnight chamber of a grouse,
crouched over like some bear
digging for honey
I discover gold!
Not the first time
I've excavated a *kieppi*
but another lesson in reality,
forgotten the cold
the fury of my anxieties
pushed aside like the snow
blocking this tunnel entrance.
All is revealed...
silent plunge into snow at dusk
silent waiting rest beneath
emergence at dawn, feather marks
from the first flurry of flight.
The bed is marked by a
double handful of clean droppings
golden-brown, evenly-formed
expressed fibrous remains
easily lifted intact together
with a layer of frozen snow
solidified by body heat.
The upper layer of droppings
appears molten, melted
then congealed...held up to
the sunlight their smooth surface
shows some puzzling striated
patterns, like a mineral
fine impressions...
feathers of gold.

FAREWELL TO WINTER

When snowdrifts dwindle overnight
horned larks arrive and
crows frolic in flocks,
when kids claim freedom on bikes
hunched over against roads yet soft,
when old men stand firmly
measuring yard chores,
while cows drop quivering calves
in steaming pastures
and deer walk about high
surprised by free feet, then
I feel a slow drawing down
and reflect on winter's joys.

I did not think to
see winter end so soon, but
now I blink, surprised by sunlight
reflecting from roadside pools
yet icebound but soon to shrink,
and note that dry grass beckons
though too damp beneath to comfort
and all the world's gone from white
to dull hues of brown and tan,
or black where fields emerge,
though willows blaze yellow and red
the last patches of snow making
a final statement against their color
an epitaph to cold wind and
hard frozen ground where mice shelter
shivering under shadows
and lick wet feet.

My heart balances between the ecstasy
of a harrier's mad plunging and vibrant rise,
the delight of children thrusting sticks
in soft ice to see the water rise and
join the flood of stream gathering
to leave the land behind while
sullen smoke rises as grassfires turn
tan to black presaging green...
the land renewed again, warm, still.

NEW DAY

Crazed at dawn
small birds fly
into another day
gleeful as children
before a party.

They plunge through
the cool air
with ardent wings
and muffled cries.

WET FOX

It bounded across the road
on small dark silent feet
in the headlights of the car ahead—
for just a moment I tensed
fearing to see it tossed aside
another decrepit bit of litter
but it slipped through a space
of time held breathless
leaving me a clear image of
wet matted fur dishevelled, muddied
I guessed, by February thaw
that blurred our windshields,
the fields sodden mats of snow
and mud like felt in patches,
fox running lone in the night
shanks thin as wires and that
great toss its tail tattered,
this I saw before it vanished—
one long winter pursuing prey
brought nearly to a close,
mice tormented by icy crusts
now bewildered in the damp,
spring's urge upon the land,
the mice, the fox and I.

TREE FEATHER

A lone tall tamarack
at the edge of the bog
on a cold April night
like a gray owl's
tail feather
spread flat against
the starlit sky.

ENCOUNTER

"Look, a harrier", I cried,
pointing to the great bird
stealthily gliding toward us
across creekside rushes on
long motionless wings V-set
on a level rising plane...
as I spoke, it flared,
pivoting on one dropped wing
to meet a chance warbler
fleeing from its lean shadow;
with spread tail the harrier
turned to intercept its prey,
rising up before us,
awhirl with flailing wings,
mounting the air with the
adroit elegance of a
morning kingbird fast upon
a shimmering dragonfly;
twice it turned upon the
darting, driven warbler, then,
startled to find us there,
it swept away upstream—
leaving us enthralled.

A FALL OF ASPENS

They call it trembling aspen
but I am trembling
set to mumbling with glee
who came to see
the autumn woods
to watch the aspens turn
that marvelous trick
going almost overnight from
sombre green to twinkling yellow—
though now I recall
how in spring those
leaflets danced another tune
making music off their twigs
a joyful dance of delight.

Even before there were leaves
our aspens took my breath
dripping with silvered catkins
glowing in the early light
while sapsuckers foraged quietly
among those draped delights
a new world building at
treetop's heights
the sun holding fast
sap springing.

Oaks shed leaves brown and twisted
as rusted tin but
aspen leaves lie flat
supple and smooth
yellow velvet disks
laid to rest in solemn fall
a gentle rain of colour
that lets in the blue sky
where pale trunks stand tall
and grouse hold motionless
exposed to view

thrilled to see so far—
a shocking feathered explosion
setting aspen leaves awhirl.

Even at dusk
their fallen leaves gather light
brightening shadowy roadsides
lifting our spirits as we
drive down gravel roads
bordered with woods...
a hush at twilight
a glow beyond the trees
where leaves blanket the grass
one leaf upon another.

In all the woods
I see no bounty greater
than those congealed drops
of last night's cold rain
shining silver spheres still
on each gold leaf's level top
drawing in the fearsome light
of October sun at dawn
pressed beneath my shoe
in calm disregard of
heaven's bent...
who'd gladly gather them in and
drink a toast to birds that
sip such nectared fall
with mincing grace
and peer aloft in fright
when swift shadows strike...
a hawk's passing marked
by each beating heart
juncos standing fast...
the sharp-shin faster still.

I wouldn't trade the eastern
maple's red for our
aspen's golden hue
though where dogwood's crimson
drapery depends
aspens glow more fully
just as spruce pressed upon
their flanks build banks
of ochre ore
a feast for pallid thoughts
and green-burned vision,
but against the blue of
autumn sky, I swear,
such molten yellow
never grew but blossomed—
how from summer's green
came these twinkling sunlets
burst upon our trees
with autumn's gladness?

THE HUNT

The morning was in our grasp
when you pointed out geese
I hadn't heard
two skeins high in
a blue vaulted sky against
feathery clouds higher still,
father and son looking up:
"Hardly geese, just specks"
I muttered, urging us back to
our labored grouse hunt—
now I recall the still air
bare aspen limbs gleaming
pungent scent of leaves
the warmth between us—
we should have stopped then
to rest the panting dog
and gather more fully
what we already had.

GREY NOVEMBER DAY

Somewhere in the woods
this grey November day
there are butterflies
sleeping, hiding, still...
I've looked for them,
peeled loose bark off trees
sifted through fallen leaves
turned over rotted logs
wondering if I'd know one
if one fell out, drab
leaflike, motionless
bright colours hidden
between folded wings.

The woods are damp, cold
it is almost snowing
but here in spring butterflies
will arise from long sleep
and dance along the path
on sparkling wings.

One day I'd like to follow a
butterfly to its hiding place
watch it slowly make its way
to some secret bower
creeping out of sight
curling its legs together
opening and closing its
wings one final time
in a silent sigh.

Robert and Ruth Nero

BIOGRAPHY

Robert Nero, a native of Wisconsin, has lived in Canada since 1955. He is the acknowledged North American authority on the Great Gray Owl and the author of the book *The Great Gray Owl - phantom of the northern forest.*

Virtually every area of natural history is of interest to Bob Nero. He has a meticulous eye for detail and the ability to discover simple common sense explanations for apparently complex problems. Never too busy to correspond with amateur naturalists, he has encouraged many young people in their interest in biology and natural history, and is well known for his nature writings, which have appeared in many popular magazines and journals.

The Ernest Thompson Seton Award, presented by the Manitoba Naturalists Society in 1981 for outstanding achievement in the field of natural history, recognizes his extensive contribution to the natural history of Manitoba, and the prairie region.

Following twenty productive years as Senior Ecologist with theWildlife Branch of the Manitoba Department of Natural Resources, Bob Nero retired in May 1991 but retains an office as volunteer Senior Ecologist.

The sketches in this book are reproduced courtesy of Winnipeg artist, James A. Carson. The publishers also acknowledge the cooperation of the Manitoba Department of Natural Resources. Jim Carson's lively drawings also illustrate *Woman by the Shore and other Poems* published in 1990 by Natural Heritage, Toronto.

www.ingramcontent.com/pod-product-compliance
Lightning Source LLC
Chambersburg PA
CBHW071641050426
42443CB00026B/799